The Young Adult Starter Kit

12 STEPS To Being A Better Person

Ben Povlow

THE YOUNG ADULT STARTER KIT

12 STEPS TO BEING A BETTER PERSON

BEN POVLOW

THE SELF-HELP COMPANY, LLC.

CHECK OUT BEN'S PODCAST

Available in all major podcast directories

The Young Adult Starter Kit: 12 Steps To Being A Better Person

Copyright © 2021 by Ben Povlow

All rights reserved.

No part of this publication may be reproduced, stored in a retrieval system, or transmitted in any form or by any means (electronic, mechanical, photocopying, recording or otherwise) without prior written permission of the publisher. For permission requests, contact:

The Self-Help Company, LLC. 1457 Kelly Road #255 Apex, NC. 27502

While efforts have been made to verify the information contained in this publication, neither the author nor the publisher assumes any responsibility for errors, inaccuracies, or omissions. All readers are advised to seek professionals related to specific situations. The reader of this publication assumes responsibility for the use of this information.

ISBN # 978-1-7354223-6-7

To my wife, Kathi, and my step-daughter, Katelyn, thank you both for all your love and support.

Contents

Introduction	I
1. Step 1 - Personal Responsibility	1
2. Step 2 - Confidence	10
3. Step 3 - Courage	17
4. Step 4 - Faith	25
5. Step 5 - Purpose	32
6. Step 6 - Mindset	42
7. Step 7 - Attitude	51
8. Step 8 - Self-Esteem	59
9. Step 9 - Goals	68
10. Step 10 - Procrastination	84

11. Step 11 - Positive Thinking	94
12. Step 12 - Self-Image	102
Book Excerpt - Self-Help for At-Risk Teens	109
About The Author	116

Introduction

There is a saying *if it's going to be, it's up to me*. Please take a minute to give some thought to this phrase because almost everything you must do is up to you as an independent adult. Once you get to the point in your life when there's no one around to do it for you, you're not going to have a choice. So take responsibility for what you can control.

The 12 steps covered in this book are all focused on topics in which you have total control. Each chapter will move you one step closer to overall happiness and fulfillment. Everyone has a choice to work towards becoming the best possible version of themselves or remain the same. Learn how to get better results with what you already possess. Then, become the best version of yourself by applying the practical information covered throughout the pages ahead.

I understand that there is always some level of discomfort associated with change. There will be things that will feel unnatural for you to do, and that's okay because you will overcome these challenges and become a better person in the process. You will have the courage to be yourself and have faith that the results will work out in your favor when you live a purposeful life. The more prepared you are, the better chance you have of overcoming the challenges of life that we all face every day.

Becoming an independent, self-reliant person gives you the ability to be true to yourself without having to worry about what other people think about you. You came into this world by yourself, and you are going to leave this world by yourself. If you're fortunate enough to have people helping you along the way, that's great. But in some cases, you will not have that support or guidance. So, the more you can learn on your own and do for yourself, the better off you're going to be. Of course, having the skills to do things independently doesn't mean you always will have to do it by yourself, but it's nice to know you can if you have to.

When you have total control over how you live your life, you won't worry about what other people think of you because you will be living life on your terms. Making positive decisions and choices for yourself is the first step in taking control of your life. Then, doing what you know will serve you better moving forward will put you on a path to independence.

For example, taking a job because you think it's right for you and not because of what other people think will be good for you. Choosing for yourself means going to school and getting an education when your friends are skipping class and hanging out behind the bleachers or chilling out at a coffee shop when they should be in school. You are not alone in facing these situations, but you can separate yourself from the pack by choosing to make decisions based on what is best for your future and not because of what seems to be cool at the moment.

Becoming the best version of yourself means making the hard decisions because they are what's best for you—not being a follower. Becoming a leader and doing what you know will make you a stronger person and serve you better in the future. Becoming a better person means doing what's uncomfortable. Get out of your comfort zone and challenge yourself. You can do much more than you give yourself credit for.

Life is not a dress rehearsal; you only get one shot. You must get in the game. You cannot win the game of life by sitting in the bleachers. You can't sit back and wait for life to happen. Be aggressive and have a plan. Set goals and have an action plan to achieve those goals if you want to live an above-average life. You control your destiny by the small choices you are making every day. Play the game of life to win.

I understand there are certain things in your life you cannot control, but there is also a lot that you can control. So I encourage you to make the decision to control everything in your power. Envision yourself winning the everyday battles you face and winning at getting good grades, winning at making new friends and winning at being successful in a job or a career.

If you are not happy with your current job, set a goal of finding a job you will enjoy and commit to keeping it for a minimum of one year. Don't keep floundering around and quitting every time something becomes difficult. Make a commitment and stick to it. Take control of stabilizing your income and develop a routine that works for you. Find time to have a life outside of school or work to enjoy your hobbies. Make time for doing things that will make you happy.

With every experience, you are learning. And by consistently learning, you are becoming a more valuable person. You never know how you will use the skills you gain from a specific job down the road. Little life experiences will help you when you least expect them. Anytime you are dealing with people, you are developing valuable people skills that can assist you in all areas of life.

Learn how to attract the right type of people to you. Show people that you care. Be compassionate and willing to help other people. If you're not that kind of person now, I understand. Sharing yourself with others is a learnable skill. Very few people succeed in life solely on their own. When you realize that you can't win big in life by being all about yourself, the question becomes, how do I attract the right people to me? The answer is you become a person of value, and the right people will be attracted to you.

Famous motivational speaker Zig Ziglar says, "when you help enough people get what they want, you can have everything in life that you want." A powerful quote. If you listen to Zig Ziglar, which I highly recommend, or read any of his books, you will hear this phrase repeatedly.

Think about how you can help others and take the focus off yourself. Choosing to give back is a decision that will reward you in ways you can't imagine. Take control of what you do with your spare time. Believe that you deserve the rewards that come along with doing right in life.

If there is something specific you have always been curious about, take the initiative to learn more about the topic. If there is a particular aspect of your life that always feels out of control, do some research on ways to improve the situation. Do some research and discover the ways other people have overcome similar challenges. Then create a customized plan to incorporate these changes into gaining control over what once seemed uncontrollable.

Become independent. Don't wait for someone else to do for you what you are capable of doing for yourself. Start the process on your own if it's important to you and then if you need help, ask someone. Think outside the box and find ways to create leverage using the abundance of tools and resources available to you. When you feel stuck, seek out information that will help you find a breakthrough and get you to that next level.

These are all ways that you can help yourself take control of your life. And as you become a better person, the world around you will become better. When you focus on thinking and acting positively, taking control of your life becomes so much easier.

You will be amazed by the feeling of independence you receive when you take control of your life and make the independent choices that create lasting happiness. Being willing to accept personal responsibility and choosing not to make excuses is vital to your quest to becoming the best possible version of yourself. Welcome positive change into your life. Be open to endless possibilities and dream big.

Step 1 - Personal Responsibility

Personal responsibility is all about not making excuses for things in which you can control. If you make a mistake, own it, and learn from the experience. Living a fulfilling life starts with you. Blaming others for what you have or don't have will not improve your situation.

If you want a prosperous life, having the courage to accept responsibility is part of the foundation. Even when the outcomes are not great, or the situation you're in may make you look bad, you cannot make excuses and blame others. If something is not how you want it to be, stop complaining and do something about it.

When it comes to situations in your life where you're unhappy, not getting the results you desire or if you fail at something and things didn't go your way, complaining and blaming won't help you. Focus on what you did and how you could have done it differently to learn from the experience. Everyone makes mistakes, everybody goes through tough times, and everyone makes bad decisions.

Refuse to complain about how someone has done you wrong and focus on how you can avoid having this happen to you again. Blaming is just another form of making an excuse. Accepting personal responsibility means not making excuses or playing the blame game. Thinking that it is okay for you to blame other people or to blame a particular situation or blame a circumstance for what's going on in your life will only perpetuate your willingness to blame and make excuses.

Do your best to avoid comparing yourself to other people. We are all different in one way or another. Your situation being different doesn't make you better or worse than the next person. Accept yourself for who you are.

You can control your circumstances by making better decisions. By making excuses, you're giving yourself the easy way out instead of trying to figure out how you could improve the situation or make it better. Failing to plan is planning to fail. So, create a plan for improving the various parts of your life you are not happy with.

Set your goals and plan to achieve them. The way you do that is by creating an action plan. When you have a specific goal, don't give yourself excuses to get out of doing the work. Don't accept excuses from yourself. We will talk more about goals in a later chapter of this book.

For example, when it comes to your physical health and wanting to exercise more, it's easy to give yourself excuses of saying I'm too tired, I had a long day at work or school, so I'm going to pass on it today. The thing is, when you start to give yourself these excuses, and you accept them, you will continue to have that escape hatch, and you will think you can give yourself that excuse every time the conditions aren't perfect. Before you know it, it's been thirty days, sixty days, or ninety days since you did the thing you set out to do. Understand, putting off what is important to you will become a never-ending cycle if you can't stop yourself from making excuses. When it comes to personal improvement, if you don't hold yourself accountable, nobody else will.

Developing new habits and accomplishing your goals will require commitment. Committing means not wavering regardless of what obstacles get in your way. Commitment is figuring out how to overcome difficulties, get around them, push through them, and do what you set out to do, even when the conditions are not ideal.

When you know why you're doing something, it will motivate you to keep going when you're ready to give up or put off what is important to you. Having the reason you are doing something fresh in your mind will keep you from making excuses and give you the strength to push forward even when you're tired or don't feel well. Some days you will have to get creative with your time. If you know you will be exhausted at the end of the day, consider doing your most important task first thing in the morning. Wake up an hour earlier than usual if that is what it takes to stay committed to the promise you made to yourself.

Pace yourself throughout the day. Create a schedule that you know will work for you so there won't be any reason to make excuses for why you can't fulfill your commitments. When your tasks are important to you, and nobody else can do them for you, the pressure to perform will provide the motivation needed to accept the personal responsibility and do what needs to be done. Think about the pain of not doing your thing. Imagine how not getting it done will affect you. If you said you would do something, be a person of your word and get it done.

If you will not accept excuses from yourself, why would you accept them from other people? If somebody says they're going to do something, hold them accountable. If you start hearing the same excuses from a person repeatedly, you should begin to realize this person has issues with keeping their word. If you accept their excuses, they will continue giving them to you. Paying attention to how often other people are making excuses will help you see how big of a problem it can be.

One way you can learn to avoid making excuses is to have an accountability partner. An accountability partner is somebody who is doing a similar thing to what you are doing, and you hold each other accountable for doing what you each said you would do by a specific day or time. Accountability partners are most commonly seen in people who go to the gym together. For example, a gym buddy is someone that agrees to meet you every night at six o'clock at the gym. If they are expecting you to be there, it provides motivation for you to go even when you don't feel like doing it because you don't want to leave your partner hanging.

If you find yourself with an accountability partner, who is always giving you excuses and says, well, I can't go today because I was up late and I'm tired. If you accept that as an excuse from them, now you might be tempted to say, okay, well, I guess I don't have to go either. Reliability is a crucial part of picking the right person to team up with. No excuses for you means going by yourself if your partner cancels because you're committed to your goals, regardless of what other people do.

Focus on what you can control personally, not what other people control for you. This was just an example of how having an accountability partner works. You can do this for any area of your life in which you know someone who has similar goals as you.

Don't accept excuses for not doing the thing that you have total control over. Tell yourself the truth, set realistic goals. If you say that you want to lose a certain amount of weight, then you need to do a certain number of things when it comes to eating right and exercising.

Be honest with yourself. Do you think this is a realistic goal? Don't make excuses and say, I said I was going to lose twenty pounds, and it's been a month, and I've only lost one, so, I guess it's not even worth it, and then you give up. Set smaller goals, have them be to only lose five pounds in a month if that's what it takes, but be honest and realistic with yourself when setting goals. Break your goals down into smaller bite-sized chunks so that they are doable to remove any excuse of why they can't be accomplished.

When you say you're going to do something, hold yourself accountable. Be honest with yourself and commit to doing it regardless of who else is with you. And be patient so that when times do get tough, you won't be too hard on yourself. Pace yourself and know that you will eventually achieve your goal if you're doing a little bit every day. If you make your goals too big, it will discourage you if you don't reach them. To avoid giving yourself the excuse of something being too hard to do, break it down into manageable steps that you can take to increase your progress gradually. Make a total commitment to whatever it is you are setting out to do.

Don't be scared to do the work. Don't be afraid to fail. Don't give yourself excuses as to why you can't do it. Focus on reasons why you can do it. Believe in yourself and your abilities, and you will be more confident. When you're more confident, you will be more motivated. When you're motivated, you will get more done.

It's easy to make excuses for anything in life. But the people who are willing to push through, do the hard work, and not make excuses are the ones who achieve the most. I want you to achieve maximum results in your life. I want you to overcome all the odds. I want you to prove everybody wrong regarding what they said you can or can't do.

The most important thing you need to do is accept personal responsibility for the things you can control and avoid making excuses. Don't make excuses when things go wrong, don't make excuses when you don't do what you said you were going to do. If you don't do what you said you would do, admit that you messed up and recommit. Say, I'm going to try again; this time, I'm going to do it. Please don't be ashamed about it.

If you say you're going to do something and you don't, just go back and do it later if it's possible. Unless it's a time-sensitive thing and you missed the opportunity. If so, say, I accept the responsibility, and

I won't let it happen again. You can't make excuses by saying, "oh, I didn't do it because this happened or that happened." If somebody said they would give you a million dollars to do it, I bet you would find a way. And that's the way you need to think of everything in your life, big or small.

What is the reward? Why are you doing it? You can reward yourself for every little task you have to achieve. Reward yourself, make it worth it. No excuses, get it done and then reward yourself. I want you to have everything you want in your life, and it all starts with not making excuses.

Throughout this book, you will learn a wide range of motivational, informational, and practical personal development and self-help strategies that you can use to take your life from where you are now to where you want to go. The next chapter is all about Confidence, which will help you in your ability to avoid making excuses and embrace personal responsibility.

Step 2 - Confidence

One of the best ways you can ensure that you are creating a life that doesn't suck is to develop your confidence. Build on the confidence that you already have and believe in yourself. Doing this will give you the feeling that you can do anything you put your mind to.

Much of what you can do is based on the level of confidence you have in yourself. If you do not believe in yourself, you hinder your ability to succeed in any area that you're focused on. Believing in yourself and knowing you can do it will help you achieve whatever goals you set for yourself.

Without this self-confidence, you will be hesitant to go after what you want in your life. A lack of self-confidence will hold you back from trying new things and keep you from setting the big goals you want to accomplish. Without believing in yourself, you may never try anything out of your comfort zone, and that is where the magic happens.

You can develop your confidence by thinking about what you have been successful at in the past, then try to relate it to what you are setting out to do now. Think about the process you went through in preparing yourself; what was it that gave you the belief to go for it? Were there people who told you that you could do it? Was it because you saw someone else do it first? Think about what gave you the belief you needed in these previous experiences.

One of the main reasons people don't believe they can do a certain thing is a lack of knowledge or skill on the topic. These hurdles can be overcome by studying and practicing. The more knowledge you have on a topic, the more confident you will become. The more you practice doing something, the easier it will be for you to get good at doing it.

Whatever area you're focusing on, whether it be health goals, financial goals, spiritual goals, educational goals, becoming good in a sport, or playing a certain musical instrument, your level of confidence will often determine your level of success. If you're low on confidence right now and you don't believe that you can do it, I'm going to help you by providing some strategies, tips, and techniques you can use to build up your confidence.

So again, have you been successful in the past? Even if it hasn't been with this particular thing, that is now your focus. Think about when you have been successful, achieved a specific goal, or have overcome a particular obstacle where you weren't sure about yourself, and you weren't confident, but you went for it anyway. If you did that in the past and overcame those obstacles, how did it turn out? Were you able to do what you sought out to do? If so, I want you to think about that experience and how you were unsure and not confident, but you did it anyway, and you were able to be successful. Use that experience as inspiration to build your confidence.

It doesn't matter if you were a young child when you had this previous success; it could have been ten years ago. If you could do it once, you can do it again if you believe in yourself and take that chance. If you are setting out to do something that you have never done before, and you have doubts about whether it's possible, here's the question I want you to ask yourself, has someone else already done whatever it is you're setting out to do? Because if someone else has been able to do it, then you know it's possible. You can use their success to build your confidence by believing if they did it, you can do it.

Now you need to learn what they did to create those successful results. Figuring out what they did may take a little research and may even require you to contact that person if that's a possibility. Ask them, what did you do to be successful at this specific thing? And in a lot of cases, people will tell you. They will be willing to help you because people are more generous than you may think. You won't know if you don't ask.

If you cannot contact a person directly, see if they have a blog post where you can make a comment, or ask a question. See if they have ever done an interview explaining their process for preparing and achieving the desired results. Maybe there is a video where they've said, here's precisely what I did, and if you follow my exact plan, you can do it too. You will be surprised at how easy it can be to find the answers to doing something once you take the time to look. When you doubt whether you can do something or not, ask yourself this question, how can I get advice on what it will take to achieve this goal?

Now that you know what you want to do is possible, focus on becoming more knowledgeable on the topic and believing in yourself. The more you know, the more confident you will become once you learn what steps will need to be taken. Most doubt comes from not knowing enough about the topic. If you desire to learn and become good at something, commit to doing what it will take. Determine what skills you need to learn, then go out and develop those skills. Practice consistently, and you will inevitably become better with each day that passes.

Commit to developing the areas of your life you want to become successful in. It doesn't matter if it's health and wellness or a physical job. Anything you want to do, you can learn how. Believe in yourself and know that all the information is out there, and you just need to seek it, learn it, and then apply it. Once you start using it, you will see small achievements and little bits of growth that will motivate you and excite you, which will build your confidence. When you see progress, it will build your belief because you see proof of what's possible.

Using affirmations is another excellent way to become more confident in yourself. Every morning when you wake up, you can envision yourself becoming good at this thing you want to do. You can affirm it to yourself and into your subconscious mind by saying, I am becoming better at this topic, at this hobby, at this skill every day. (insert the name of what it is that you're focused on) Repeat out loud; I'm becoming better every day, I am confident in myself and my ability to accomplish my goals.

Begin to see yourself at the finish line. See yourself becoming the person you want to be. Create that vision of success and believe it will happen because you're practicing and becoming more knowledgeable every day. Not just because you think it's going to magically happen but believe it because you're doing the work that's necessary for you to achieve this goal.

Practicing the techniques mentioned in this chapter will raise your confidence level of what you can accomplish. I recommend that you read, watch, listen to, and learn more about any subject or topic in which you want to become better. Knowledge and practice are the keys to building your confidence and helping you reach your true potential.

Doing new things will require you to increase your willingness to take risks and the ability to be vulnerable. Understand, you may fail at your first attempt of trying something new, but your ability to get back up and continue to learn and grow from your mistakes is what will separate you from those who quit on their dreams. Keep trying until you eventually accomplish your goal. Failing at something doesn't mean that you are a failure; it just means that you failed at this attempt. Don't be afraid to fail and try again.

In the process of developing your confidence, you will need the courage to take chances and try new things. In the next chapter, I am going to dive into the topic of courage. You will learn what it means to be willing to put yourself out there in order to grow into the person you want to become.

Step 3 - Courage

Now is the time to develop the courage to go after what you want in your life. Having the confidence of knowing that you can do it is great but having the courage to go for it is something different.

The courage to go for it ultimately means that you are willing to take calculated risks, even when you don't know what the outcomes will be. But you're willing to go for it anyway because it's what you believe is the right thing for you to do. Once you develop courage, you can use this in all areas of your life. It doesn't matter if you're talking about playing a sport or in your creative life when it comes to art, ideas, inventions, or anything you are working on or working towards that you're just unsure of and you may have some self-doubt about it.

The chapters of this book are structured in a way that each topic builds on the last. Because as you develop these different skills and take these different steps, you're building towards becoming a better person.

And having all these attributes will serve you better than just having one or the other. The more skills you have in your bag of tricks, the better off you will be because these topics go hand in hand. That's why it is best to read this entire book from beginning to end in order.

Having the courage to do anything is the willingness to put yourself out there and take chances. You know what you want to do, you just may not believe you know enough, or you may not understand enough about it to be confident. So, once you develop that confidence, you must have the courage to take the action and put yourself out there and be willing to be seen for who you are because you are unique and capable.

Courage is what gives you the ability to go after what you want, regardless of what people will say about it, irrespective of what people might be thinking about you. Your job is to do what you believe is best for you and not worry about other people's judgments. There will always be someone who wants to judge you; that shouldn't affect whether or not you do something.

When you dare to put yourself out there, you may feel vulnerable; you may feel exposed. You may feel like people will see a side of you that they've never seen before, and you may be worried about what that might look like to other people. The courage to be yourself will play a significant role in achieving genuine happiness. Achieving your dreams will require different forms of courage along your journey.

Think about all the different musicians and actors and actresses on TV every day doing things that may be uncomfortable for them. Many of them love what they do, but it still takes courage to do it. A musician may like to play music, but it takes a lot of courage to perform in front of thousands of strangers. They do this to entertain people and create a pleasurable experience for others, but there will always be some people who don't like that musician. Some people have fans, and some entertainers have people who don't like them. The ones who have the courage to embrace their passions are most successful.

You can't worry about who's going to like or dislike what it is you do. Your job is to be yourself in a strategic way. Now, when I talk about taking risks, I'm not talking about taking foolish risks. I am talking about taking calculated risks. These are where you think about what you're going to do, you plan for what you're going to do, and then you make your move.

It's okay to make mistakes and not be perfect all the time. Being yourself means having a human experience. It means doing what you desire to do in a way that will make you happy. You must understand that nobody is perfect. People make mistakes every day. You may not see them all the time, but they're happening.

When it comes to making a movie, these actors and actresses are not perfect. It takes many tries to get a scene exactly right. You may not see the mistakes because they get edited out. But at the end of the movie, if you see the bloopers, you will see where people made mistakes. Actors are putting themselves out there and making fools of themselves in some people's eyes, but it doesn't stop them. When you think about it, in the world of acting, people are making a lot of money to embarrass themselves and to get criticized.

Some artists create artwork, whether it be a painting or any other type of art, and some people love it and there are some who hate it. The opinions of others don't stop the artist from creating their art. I'm sure you have heard the saying, *beauty is in the eye of the beholder*, and this saying is true because all forms of art are subjective. Most artists create what they enjoy, and if others like it too, that is just a bonus.

Courage is being willing to do what makes you happy regardless of what other people will think about it. Your journey begins by understanding where you are, what challenges you face, where you want to go, and how you will get there. If you feel like you don't have the courage to step out into the world and let people see you, there are ways you can develop this courage. It's similar to the way you build confidence by becoming more knowledgeable and gaining experience.

Practice being courageous. For example, if you are trying to muster up the courage to present yourself on video, you can do a test recording and watch it back to see where your mistakes are and how you can fix them—practice in private first. You don't need to jump right out into the public eye. You plan and rehearse just like actors rehearse their lines. And as you become better, you will have more confidence, and you'll start to develop the courage to publish your videos and allow people to see you in action.

Do your best not to compare yourself to others. You may want to achieve the results that they have completed but stop worrying about what others have been able to do and focus on how you can become the best version of yourself. Focus on what you really want and make a plan for how to achieve it. Then give it one hundred percent of your effort and believe in yourself. When you know you have given it your all, there will be no room for regrets.

You are unique, and the thing you want to do may have never been done before. The art you want to create has never been created before. The book you want to write has never been written before. So, it's hard to gauge where your piece of art might fit into the world, but you'll never know if you don't try.

There are also ways you can develop the courage to do your thing without having to worry about putting your name or face out there. If you want to write a book, make music, create art, or anything else you want to create, you can do it under a pen name, or a nickname, so you don't have to put your real name out there. People don't need to see your picture or know your real name to appreciate your work.

Once you develop the courage to create the work or do the thing, then you can wait to see how people react if you want to, if that's what is holding you back. Once you realize that people appreciate and enjoy what you do, you will have the courage to step out and say, it was me. I was the one who made this thing you love so much. And if you don't get the reaction or response you were hoping for, you never have to reveal yourself as the creator. Be willing to accept the feedback and make improvements so you can get better on your next attempt. There are ways to ease into things and build courage and confidence along the way.

Start with having the courage to believe that you are enough; you are enough for yourself, and you are enough for your family and the people who genuinely love you. You will be doing what's right for you, and that's what is most important. You are unique; love yourself. Appreciate yourself. Appreciate that you have special abilities and talents and be willing to put them out there for the world to see. Have the courage to take worthwhile risks and be seen for your true self.

Even when the outcomes are uncertain, your art, ideas, and creations are all things that the world needs. Be brave; go for what you want. Be courageous. Continue to develop yourself into the person you want to be. Believe that what you have to offer the world is special, go for it.

The next chapter is on faith, developing faith in yourself and the results you want but can't physically see.

Step 4 - Faith

Having faith is believing without any physical evidence or proof of the results you will achieve, but you believe good things will happen. Now that you have confidence and courage, it's time to combine them with faith and perform whatever it is you're looking to do.

In this chapter, I will provide you with strategies and ideas of how you can become more faithful in yourself and in the results you're looking to achieve. Faith builds off the other topics that were covered in the previous chapters about visualizing what you want and preparing yourself for the things you want to do. If you are working towards something with good intentions, believe you deserve the results you will achieve. Trust that the results will work out in your favor.

Now, these results may not be exactly the way you saw them, but you might be surprised that sometimes the results you desire may not even have been the best for you. It may work out for you in a different way, one you may not have been expecting or have thought of as a possibility. Understanding there are no guaranteed results, acting on faith is sometimes all you have.

To increase the chances of achieving your desired results, start by seeing them in your mind first. Then, envision yourself crossing the finish line and holding that trophy. Trust that you have prepared yourself to the best of your ability and then give it one hundred percent of your effort and have faith in the results.

You may hear people say, "this person was lucky, or that person was lucky." As I have come to know it, the definition of luck is "luck is when preparation meets opportunity." Meaning if you're preparing yourself for a particular thing and you're studying, and doing the work, when an opportunity presents itself, you will be ready to capitalize on it. And that is where you have the success. But, on the other hand, people may see it as luck because they didn't see you doing the hard work behind the scenes.

Understand that you don't always get your desired results immediately. You may not always see the benefits right away. It may take time. But when you have faith, you must be willing to be patient and know that not everything will provide instant gratification. If you go into a situation with faith and focus on the results you want with a positive mindset, you won't focus on the fears you may have. And although you may have some fears and doubts, your faith can overpower them. There may be some uncertainties, things you're worried about, or you don't know how it will work out, but those stresses will begin to dissipate when you have faith. Focus on what you can control and believe in yourself.

Believe you are knowledgeable enough and skilled enough, then have faith that the results will work out in your favor. Of course, you can't always control the results, but if you act with faith and believe it, you will give yourself the best chance to achieve the desired results. These results may not be just as you imagined, but you will never know if you don't try.

Always remember why you're doing something. Your "why" is a powerful motivator. What is your reason for wanting to do this specific thing? If you could be successful at what you want to do, how will these results change your life? Keeping a clear picture of that success in your mind will give you the faith you need to see that the benefits of the accomplishment outweigh the risk of not going for it. When you are focused on these positive results, your doubts and worries will start to fade away.

Your reason for doing different things will vary, but there is always a reason why attached to it. So try to focus on the reason why for everything you do and use it to motivate and push you towards accomplishing the task. You can use this technique for tasks big and small and in all areas of your life.

When whatever it is you're doing will help people or provide some form of value to others, you should feel good about what you are doing. If you're not looking to harm anyone or trying to deceive anybody and you are doing it with good intentions, have faith and believe something good will come from your efforts. When you are knowledgeable and well prepared like we talked about in the previous chapters, in addition to providing you with confidence and courage, this should also give you faith in what it is you're doing. When you're doing something for the right reasons and with good intentions, you should have confidence that you will receive favorable results.

Have your faith be based on the understanding that you are knowledgeable in this area. You have studied and are doing the hard work behind the scenes that people don't see. When people see others having success, for example, whether it be in sports, music, dancing, or acting, they tend to think it just happened naturally overnight without considering all the time, practice, and dedication that has taken place before the public event. Nobody sees all the practicing, rehearsing, and preparing. Most people who have success in public spend a ton of time focusing on becoming the best they can be, and they have faith that it will work out for them. Most people don't see the hard work being done when there are no cameras around. Then, after all this preparation in advance, they make it look easy when it's showtime.

People don't show you the hard work they are doing behind the scenes. All you see is the glamour and the glory when it comes to fruition. Think about it this way, if you knew the results would be in your favor, how would you act? How would you feel? How would you prepare? How would you present yourself? So, imagine the results being in your favor. Visualize it happening and see yourself being successful. And then carry yourself in the way that will bring you success in whatever you do.

Having faith doesn't automatically get you the desired outcome you're looking for, but it will give you a much better chance than you will have if you only focus on getting negative results. Be intentional and have faith in yourself. Focus on positive outcomes. If something doesn't turn out the way you wanted it to, ask yourself, what can I learn from this? How can I make something out of this anyway? How can I improve myself through this experience? What can I do differently the next time?

There is always a lesson to be learned in everything you do. So even if the results don't come out the way you want them to, you can learn from the experience. When you try again, you'll know better the next time. But you must have faith that something good will come out of it, even if it isn't exactly the way you saw it because unexpected results can still be good. Maybe you will receive a result you never thought of. It could be a result that you've never even imagined possible, and it could even be potentially better than what you imagined. Having faith is doing it, stepping up, and putting yourself out there with the best intentions.

There are a lot of things you can't control. However, envisioning the results being in your favor is something you can control. And by focusing on the positive and believing in yourself, you are giving yourself the best possible chance at success.

It's better to try and not succeed than it is not to try at all. You don't want to live in regret, always wondering what if. Try hard, work hard, prepare yourself, and you can be successful in anything you put your mind to. Have faith and believe in yourself. I believe in you. I know you can do it if you work hard, focus, apply yourself, and only think about the positive things that you want. Do not focus on what you don't want because you attract what you think about the most. So, focus on the positive, and you will attract positive to you. Have faith and believe in yourself. Don't worry about trying to control every aspect of the results; take action.

Step 5 - Purpose

Do you know what your life's purpose is and how to make the most of it? How are you supposed to fulfill it and discover what you should be doing with your time and energy? If you want to be genuinely happy, feel fulfilled and feel like you're doing something bigger than yourself, this chapter will set you on the right path.

Living your day-to-day life and going through the motions can start to feel monotonous, and it can start to get boring. And you may begin to wonder, what am I doing with my life? Thoughts like these are pretty common, so don't feel like you're the only one if these types of reflections pop into your head. Especially if you're young and don't necessarily understand what you should be doing other than going to school to get an education. Much of what we do during our younger years feel pointless, like we're wasting our time.

When you start to think about the big picture of life and think about your future, it's important to consider doing something that has meaning and purpose. Something you feel will make a difference in the world and other people's lives. The more you do that, the more joy you will feel in your own life.

Discovering your purpose may not come easy to you. It doesn't come easy to many people. For most people, it takes a lot of trial and error. It took many years for me to finally discover my purpose.

In my first book, *Self-Help for At-Risk Teens*, I went into great detail about all the challenges I faced and obstacles I had to overcome as an adolescent. So, I won't go into too much detail here, but I want to tell you the story of what it took for me to discover my purpose with the hopes that it will help you find yours.

When I was a teenager, and even before that, I was constantly getting into trouble. As a teen, many of the kids I was hanging out with were dying young. I would always think, why them, why not me? Because sometimes it was the good kids, the kids who never did anything wrong who were passing away. I was always thinking, I'm one of the worst of the group; why am I still here?

I didn't want to die young, but I'd thought it was inevitable that it would happen, but it didn't. And through all these experiences of being arrested, getting shot at multiple times, constantly using drugs and alcohol, and simply wasting away my youth, I always thought there must be a reason I continue living through all these bad experiences. Plus, I had gone through all the trials and tribulations of being raised by a single mother and having lost my dad at an early age. Then my mom passed away when I was sixteen, and I started to question why I was still alive. Why would I still be here when I didn't feel like I had much to offer.

I had struggled for years wondering what I'm supposed to be doing because going to work every day at a regular job just felt boring, monotonous, and pointless. The endless cycle of making money to pay bills year after year seemed like it would never end. Something about this didn't sit right with me. It made me think there must be more to my life than this. And I struggled with thoughts like these for years.

In recent years, I've been able to clear my head and start to analyze the thoughts and feelings I was having in my body. I focused on my gut feelings and this sense of uneasiness that I couldn't shake. I felt like I should be doing something, but I didn't know what it was. I constantly had these same thoughts coming into my mind, but I couldn't make sense of them. I would be thinking to myself, man, you've been through so much, there has to be a story here worth telling. It wasn't until I started to focus on those same thoughts that would come into my head all the time that I began to get some sense of what I should be doing.

I began to ask myself, why am I thinking this exact thought all the time? These thoughts for me were, you overcome so much, what's the lesson, and how can I share it with people to help them avoid making the same mistakes? You were able to get away from the drugs; you were able to stop drinking alcohol; you were able to learn how to avoid getting into trouble. I learned my lessons and moved on to living a simple, trouble-free life; now what? What's the lesson to be shared? I started to think that by sharing my story with other people, I could help them accomplish the same goals I had while I was struggling. That's what I believe is my purpose.

I started to think about what I did to overcome my challenges and what I learned through my years of studying personal improvement, and I began to get a vision of how I would share my message. I start to think, wow, if I could go back and do it all over again, here's how I would do it, this is what I wish I had known. The idea of writing a book was something that continued to reemerge into my mind for quite a while. But I kept thinking it was crazy, so I kept dismissing this idea.

I went to see a medium, a psychic medium, for a reading. Shortly into this reading, the guy asked me if I am a writer. And at the time, the only thing I could think of was that I had written a very short story about my mom's legacy in a book that was published almost a decade earlier in 2009.

The guy says, "no, it seems much more prominent." He says, "when I see a feather, it means that you are a writer, or you should be a writer." And I said, "well, I have had thoughts about writing a book." Then he asks, "what were they about?" And I said, "they're about me sharing my own life experiences and what I've been through and how I could help other people by sharing my story." Then he says, "I believe it's in your soul to write this book." And that stuck with me.

After that day, it just kept coming into my head, "you need to write a book." His words of "it's in your soul to do this" really stuck with me.

Even though I was constantly thinking about it, I put off taking any action for months. And then, even after I got started, I only did a little bit and stopped. But the thoughts of doing the writing never stopped. So, I asked myself, "what if the stuff this guy said was true, and it really was meant to be? What did I have to lose?" I decided to have faith and commit to learning how to write and publish a book with the hopes of helping other people.

I had this uneasy feeling for months; it was almost like nerves when I was sitting around doing everyday work and basic stuff. And it just didn't feel like what I was doing was enough. I started to think that maybe if I write out some of my ideas on paper, my thoughts will become clear. I began to build a list of ideas, and the more I did it, the more everything started to make sense. Once I got started, I quickly felt like if I could organize these ideas and stories and put them out there in the right way, they will provide real value for the people who would read them. And that's basically how my first book came about.

When I was suppressing those thoughts and feelings, I was miserable. But once I began to write these thoughts out and go through the process, those feelings started to go away, and I became more excited about what I was doing. So basically, the feelings meant something. That little uneasy feeling I had when I wasn't fulfilling my purpose told me to do what I was thinking about. And if you ignore these types of feelings or thoughts, you'll never know what could have been.

Maybe the first thing you're thinking about might not be the one, but it might lead you to your purpose. So, if you have the same thoughts or ideas coming into your mind constantly, day after day, month after month, and year after year, it's worthwhile to begin paying attention to them. If something keeps weighing on you, give it a try, as long as it is with good intentions. Take action and see what happens, and then if you realize this wasn't the right thing, you can shift your focus to some of the other thoughts that are weighing on your mind.

Begin to trust your instincts and follow your gut feelings. Your purpose could be anything; you could be a dedicated animal lover, and helping animals in some way could be your thing. You might want to start by volunteering at a shelter. You may have lost a friend or family member to a specific disease or condition, and you're passionate about wanting to help find a cure or create awareness so that other people don't have to go through a painful experience. Your purpose could be to create awareness.

Your purpose isn't something you make up; it comes from within you. It may not be something you're interested in right now. It might not be a current hobby. It could be but hobbies are more along the lines of having a passion for something. Your purpose could be something that you have never thought of or are not thinking about yet. That is why it's essential to pay attention to those intuitive feelings you are having.

If there is a reoccurring theme, begin to research it and think about how it could play a part in your life. Think about what you can do to pursue it. Once you start to do that, if you begin to get passionate about it, then you know you're on the right track.

Is this new idea something you would do even if you didn't get paid for it? Are you starting to feel excited? Are you doing this for the greater good of other people? Because it can't just be about you. If it is only about you and you're the only one benefiting, then it's most likely not your purpose. Think about who else will benefit and continue to take steps towards fulfilling that purpose every day. If you're focused on the right thing and you are on the right track, maybe that uneasy feeling will start to disappear. And then, if you stop and the anxious feelings come back, perhaps that means you should get back to what you were doing.

Fulfilling your passions and purposes will lead you to happiness. And when you're doing what you love, and you see smiles on other people's faces, and you're getting compliments that what you're doing is helping other people, this is when you will start to experience true joy and happiness. Once you discover what it is you're meant to be doing, commit to it. When you realize you're on the right track, you don't want to stop. You don't want to lose that momentum.

You can have different purposes for different areas of your life. The key is to get crystal clear on exactly what your purpose is in each area of your life. Nothing becomes vibrant until it is clear. Dedicate some time and energy to discovering your purpose. How will you ever be able to fulfill your purpose if you don't know what it is?

Step 6 - Mindset

This chapter is all about developing a mindset for success and happiness. Your mindset is the attitude and outlook you have for your life or any situation within it. You may have been raised to believe that there are limitations on what's possible for you to accomplish.

Have you ever been told that you will never be able to have a specific type of job or only ever be able to achieve a certain income level? Growing up, when you talked about wanting to attend college, do you remember hearing family members say things like, "nobody in our family has ever gone to college, so what makes you so special?" These limitations have been placed on your subconscious mind and may have led you to believe that since no one else in your family has done it, you may as well not even bother trying.

If your goal is to become a self-reliant individual who creates a life that doesn't suck, you will have to ditch this old-fashioned way of thinking. You will need to step into your power and start believing new things about yourself and what you can do. Creating the life of your dreams begins with taking responsibility for what you can control. Constantly blaming other people for what you have or don't have must stop today! It's nice to have the positive support of loved ones telling you that you can become anything you want in life, but if you don't, tell it to yourself. Start believing in yourself and don't settle for average results.

People may tell you to just get a good job and keep it forever so you can have financial security, but if you have dreams of becoming an entrepreneur, I say go for it. Take a chance and bet on yourself to win at something big. That conservative mindset of just having enough and never wanting more is a limiting belief of yesteryear. We are living in the technology age where anything is possible. If you can dream it, you can do it! This optimistic way of thinking may not come naturally to you, but it is possible to develop. If you have been raised in a conservative mindset environment, it takes a little bit of work, a lot of practice, and some serious soul searching to believe that you can do much more than what you thought was possible.

After graduating from school, even if you get a good job, you shouldn't think that your education is over. As time goes on, you may be forced to seek out new income levels to keep up with the cost of inflation. You can always benefit from gaining specialized knowledge. Whether you want to eventually climb the corporate ladder or advance your career to new and evolving fields, having a future-based mindset will keep you from getting stuck in the trap of creating a boring life that will inevitably start to suck.

If you were raised with a conservative mindset and you want to develop a prosperous mindset, it's like flipping a mental switch that will take you from poverty to prosperity. Your income level or the type of money you come from isn't the point here. It's not about financial numbers; it's more about your belief system. When you start to develop a prosperity consciousness, you will see opportunities in a whole new light.

Once you commit your focus to achieving a more significant, prosperous lifestyle, you will begin to attract these things to yourself. Once you cast that vision and believe in yourself and the possibilities, it's going to require some changes on your part. These changes will be in the form of how you are spending your time, who you're spending it with, and what you put into your mind. You will need to begin sacrificing some of what you are doing now for something much better later. The prosperity mindset is most effective when you are willing to learn new things in order to achieve new heights.

See yourself becoming the person you want to be and visualize the lifestyle you want to create. Whether you desire to become married and have children, the type of house you want to live in, the location of where you want this house to be, the car you want to drive, or the amount of money you want to earn, you must believe their attainment is possible. Your level of belief will determine the chances of you achieving these dreams, not how many people tell you it's not possible.

You may have been told that no one's ever going to want you, and you'll never find anybody to put up with your stuff. And you may believe these lies at this moment but understand that it doesn't make it true just because someone told it to you. You must believe that you can attract the right person. These are the type of things that apply to every part of your life. Don't let other people determine what value you can bring to the world. It doesn't matter if someone tells you that you're not smart enough or you're not this, or you're not that. These are other people's beliefs about you; it doesn't mean you have to think about yourself that way.

Be willing to become the best version of yourself, someone who will attract great people to you, so you can create the family you want and give yourself the best chance of living a happy and enjoyable lifestyle. Having a prosperous mindset will help you create a vision and belief that your dreams are possible. Believe you deserve it and fight for your happiness. Being willing to make small sacrifices now, for more extraordinary things later, is one of the most intelligent decisions you can make for yourself.

The mindset that you will graduate and get a diploma, or a degree will help you get through those tough times or the days when someone is trying to peer pressure you into doing something that you shouldn't be doing. Because when you have the mindset that graduating is more important than anything else, you will do what it takes to eliminate the distractions and complete your goal of graduating.

How you handle these types of pressure in your younger years will set the tone for the rest of your life because as you get older, you will face similar challenges but just in different forms. As you get older, it will be your friends trying to get you to go out drinking when they know you must work the following day or someone trying to talk you into spending your rent money on concert tickets or some other shiny object. When you have a clear picture of what you want your life to look like, you won't be swayed by things that don't align with your goals and vision.

When you take full responsibility for every aspect of your life, other people's opinions of you will become less critical. When you embrace who you truly are and accept yourself regardless of any flaws you may have, this is when you will experience the sense of freedom that you have been dreaming about. There is nothing like the feeling of living life on your own terms. Become a version of yourself that nobody else has ever seen before. Create the new you!

Your belief system is your key to happiness, but it could also be your demise. Because if you believe you can do it, you can, and if you think you can't, then you won't. So, it would help if you started with the belief that anything is possible. Your potential is unknown until you try. Commit to working hard and smart to achieve the goals you set for yourself, and if you do, the vision you create will always be possible. If you hit some stumbling blocks, learn from your mistakes, make adjustments and keep pushing forward. Don't let other people tell you what you can and can't achieve.

One way you can determine your mindset's current state is to look at how you react to certain situations. Let me give you an example; If you were to fail a big test, would you say to yourself, "I'm not smart enough, or I will never be able to learn this information?" Or do you say, "what can I learn from this failure? How can I improve my skills or gain more knowledge in the subject?" You see, the difference between these two types of responses will give you an idea of whether you have a positive or negative mindset in this situation.

A positive, prosperous mindset means you have optimism, and you believe that change is possible. And when you believe that change is possible, you're giving yourself a better chance at success. When you find yourself having a negative response to failures, and you have a pessimistic view of everything in your life that doesn't go your way, you decrease your chances of improvement and growth.

Once you have identified your current mindset, you can begin to improve it. If it is already in a good place, you can stride to make it even better. If it's not so great, you can begin to take steps towards improvement. The more you believe in yourself and your capabilities, the easier it will be to make progress. And your attitude will determine how easy or hard it is to make these changes. Having a positive attitude will give you the optimism you need to succeed. And having a negative attitude will keep you right where you are or even bring you down lower if you let it. You control your destiny through your thoughts, your belief system, and your mindset about what's possible for you in your life.

Over time, the prosperous mindset will give you the ability to change in all areas of your life. Read, learn, and explore new ideas and consider saying yes when new opportunities present themselves. I know that doing this has made a big difference in my life, and I honestly believe that this can have a significant impact on your life as well. Open your mind to new opportunities, apply the information you're learning, trust that a great life is possible, and believe that anything you dream of can come true. If you work hard, develop a creative imagination, have a vision, and avoid listening to negativity, you can do it.

The more positive information you put into your mind, the more confident you will become that a life of abundance is possible for you, regardless of what the people in your life may have told you.

Step 7 - Attitude

The level at which you can control your attitude will determine your ability to make significant changes to your life. The ability to control our minds is one of the only things we have total control over when we are born. Your ability to have complete control over your mind gives you the ability to have control over your attitude. You can improve your attitude, the way you see yourself, and how other people see you.

Your attitude will attract people to you or push people away from you. When you have a positive attitude, people can sense it and feel your positive energy. When you have a negative attitude, people can also sense that negative energy about you. Your attitude can also determine how you feel. If you catch yourself thinking that you don't care about certain things or don't care about anything, you sabotage your opportunities to become happy. If you have a negative view of your life and the world around you, even if you try to fake a positive attitude, other people will be able to sense that it's not authentic.

You can do things to ensure that you have a positive attitude and you're in a good mood throughout your day. You can start your day by waking up and thinking about the things for which you are grateful. Focus on the things you do have in your life that you can appreciate. Be thankful that you have another day to make your situation better. Be appreciative of the little things you may take for granted. Being grateful is a good start to having a positive attitude.

Learn from your mistakes. Be grateful for the adversities you face because this will push you to learn and grow as a person. Don't look at failures and setbacks as being harmful; think of them as growing experiences. Maintain a positive attitude and think of ways you can use every opportunity to improve and become a better person because of the experience. You can learn to control your internal reaction, outlook, and attitude towards any situation.

The attitude you present to the world around you and the people you interact with daily can be the difference between having a great day or a miserable one. The simplest way you can show people you are positive is to smile and say hello. If you want to take an extra step, ask how they're doing, or compliment them. If you are not doing these basic things right now, give them a try and pay attention to the responses you get. Make a mental note of how you feel throughout the day when you're polite to others versus when you're not.

If you start your day in a bad mood, it can affect your attitude towards other people. So, if something unfavorable happens first thing in the morning, it's best to try and let it go and put it behind you to avoid allowing it to snowball and affect the rest of your day. If you don't shake it off right away, you're at risk of being rude to everyone with whom you come into contact. Once you give this negative attitude to someone else, they're going to shut down their positive attitude and become rude back to you, and the cycle continues. And when you smile, say hello, and engage with people, then that positivity continues. And then you can develop a rapport and have a pleasant conversation; who knows what could come of it?

They may ask how your day is going, and you may say, "I'm not in a good mood because I can't find a job." And because you're positive, this person might say, "what a coincidence, I'm looking to hire somebody, maybe I can interview you for a job here." If you have a positive attitude, people will want to do business with you, but if you act miserable and come off as being rude you will have missed this opportunity. You can't imagine how many opportunities people miss out on because of the way they carry themselves. And they will never know because they brush them off and dismiss them as quickly as possible.

Your attitude is a choice. You can be rude, or you can be polite; it's your choice every day. Even though there may be some things going on in your life that may not be great, you don't have to let it ruin your mood all the time. You must separate and control your emotions from the bad and the good and not take out your frustrations on innocent people. When you feel good about yourself, you will become a happier person.

When you apply all the individual topics covered throughout this book, and they all start working together, and you're developing all these positive things in your life, you will get to a level of happiness you never imagined was possible. Your attitude dictates how you vibrate in the world. A positive attitude leads to positive actions and results, ultimately leading you to being a better person.

On your quest to develop a more positive outlook on life and a better attitude towards it, you can do this by avoiding negative people, places, and things. Because when you are in a negative environment and around negative people who have bad attitudes, that will begin to rub off onto you. Pay attention to how you feel after spending time in a toxic environment or with a pessimistic person. Also, pay attention to how you feel after being around an uplifting situation or person. If you do this, you will immediately see how easily your attitude is affected by your surroundings.

Start to read encouraging books, watch and listen to information that will educate, motivate, and inspire you. Doing this will help you develop a better outlook on the possibilities for your life and enhance your ability to create a winning attitude. Being more optimistic will help you become happier and lift your spirits, and your mood will rise with it. When you start to think, "wow, this is possible, something good can happen for me," then you'll have a better attitude about other areas of your life as well.

When you're surrounded by negativity all the time, you will attract negative people and situations to yourself. If you're angry and your attitude shows it, you will attract other angry people, fueling your anger and perpetuating the cycle.

But the same goes for the opposite. If you're happy and positive, you'll attract happy and positive people to you. People who want to help you and see you succeed will begin to gravitate to you. Once you start to alter your approach to life, begin to smile more, and open up to people, you will be amazed at the quality of people who become attracted to you. You will have people asking you questions like, "why are you so happy today?"

People always want to know more about happy stuff; they don't want to hear more about negativity. People will be more genuinely interested in you when you have a better attitude and when you're more positive in the way you talk. When you smile, greet people, and use your manners, it will get noticed. Try this out, even when you are having a bad day, even when you don't want to, and you will be amazed by the results.

Your attitude can be controlled by the way you set the tone of your day. So, when you first wake up in the morning, consider saying some prayers or repeating positive affirmations to yourself about how today will be a good day. You can say things like; I'm going to do well today, I'm going to be happy today, I'm going to smile more today, and say them out loud to yourself in the morning to help set the tone of your day.

You can also use gratitude affirmations by saying things like, I'm happy for having another day to improve my life. I'm grateful for the opportunity to have a job. I'm happy to have good people in my life; I am thankful for the house I live in and the food I have to eat. Think about the little things you may sometimes take for granted and take a couple of minutes to be thankful for what you have. And then throughout your day, if you encounter some negativity, walk the other way, and try not to engage in it.

Another way to keep a good attitude is when you talk to someone, don't focus on their negative qualities; focus on what is positive about them. You can train your mind to only see the good in people and situations. So instead of thinking, that is an ugly shirt, you could give them a positive compliment and say, your hair looks nice today, or I love your shoes. There are a million examples; whatever it is, focus on the positive aspects and attributes of the people you come into contact with throughout your day. Be encouraging to other people because, in turn, people will be more encouraging to you.

Practice these small disciplines daily, fight the urge to have negative thoughts towards other people. Avoid thinking negative about yourself; strive to only focus on the positive. It will give you more confidence, and it will make you feel better, and when you feel better, your attitude will improve. Positivity is contagious; starting with small things will help improve other areas of your life as a by-product.

In the next chapter, we're going to talk about ways you can build up your self-esteem. As you may have noticed, this book is a series of topics related to each other. By applying each of these small strategies, they will become one big overall way of life. Together they will help you overcome many of the small obstacles that you face in your life and help you become a well-rounded, happy and successful adult. The more you take action, the better your results will be.

Step 8 - Self-Esteem

The way you see yourself, treat yourself, and the respect you show yourself, your body, and your mind have a lot to do with how you feel. Because you are important, you deserve to be treated with respect, not only by others but also by yourself.

Sometimes we let other people get to us, get under our skin, or get into our heads, and we often wonder, am I good enough? Then we start to doubt our worth because of what other people may say about us or to us. So, how can we control our level of self-esteem? It all starts with what we're putting into our mind, what we are focusing on most, and how we are spending our time.

If this is an issue for you, place a higher value on yourself and stop worrying about what other people think of you. Don't worry about what other people have, and continue to focus on becoming the best version of yourself. The goal is to feel good about yourself, feel confident in yourself, regardless of what anyone else has, says, or does.

Learn to control your attention and what you're putting into your mind. One of the biggest challenges many people are facing right now is social media. There are so many platforms right in the palm of our hands that can be so hard to resist sometimes. For example, suppose you are active on social media, and posting pictures, memes, videos of yourself, or you make posts talking about yourself or things going on in your life, people will comment. The comments people make can sometimes be rude and obnoxious and can upset you at times. These comments can get your mind spinning and cause all kinds of crazy thoughts.

There are people that you may not even know who are commenting negative things about you for whatever reason. There may be people saying that you're not good enough, or even much meaner things. It's happening every day to people all around the world. Some people are just obnoxious with the negativity on social media. All of this can be negatively affecting your self-esteem without you even realizing it. So be proactive and find ways to separate yourself from the toxic people or platforms trying to bring you down.

In contrast, if you have people that are being overly positive with what they are saying, that can be great, but it can also contribute to overblown self-esteem. So, it goes both ways with social media. When you decide to put things out into the public eye, you're opening yourself up to criticism, some good and some bad. The one thing you want to keep in mind is that if you don't know a person, especially if you've never met them a day in your life, be careful not to take their input too seriously. Because they don't know the real you and their negativity could start to cause you to have doubts about yourself when they have no idea what they're talking about.

Now, if somebody knows you personally, and they know you really well, and they're giving you criticism, then maybe you want to consider what they're saying. Evaluate yourself and what they are talking about and ask yourself some serious questions, like, am I being over the top? Am I being arrogant? Am I being cocky?

Or, if you have low self-esteem and you're making posts about being depressed or saying that you're not good enough and being down on yourself, if someone is trying to lift you up, let them. If somebody knows you personally, and they're saying you're better than this, you can do better than this, and they're encouraging you, that's the type of people you want in your life. You want to focus on and pay more attention to these people because they're the ones that care. They are giving you honest criticism, and you can use this to make the necessary changes needed to help boost your self-esteem. They want you to feel better about yourself. They are the kind of friends you want in your life. People who are positive and encouraging are the best people to spend your time with.

Another thing to consider when making posts on social media, are there people who automatically praise you for every little thing you do and immediately say how great you are? Sometimes that's a little overkill. That's kind of like having a yes, man. Somebody who's always going to agree with you no matter what you do or say, and that's not always helpful either because you can't learn and grow when you're getting biased feedback. Having people always agreeing with you can lead to overblown self-esteem, often referred to as an inflated ego or a big head.

If you're putting yourself out there on social media, be careful about the type of feedback to which you allow yourself to react. Try not to overreact or under-react; keep an open mind about what people say. If you get overwhelmed, log out of your accounts and take a break from social media for a while.

If social media is not an issue and your facing challenges in other areas of your life that are causing you to have low self-esteem, there are ways you can boost yourself up. Consider meditating, focus on living in the moment and focus on what makes you happy. Concentrate your attention on what you're good at doing. Create a list of things that you know have made you happy in the past, then do them again. Think about all your successes. Starting to think of times when you did have a lot of fun, or you were doing well in school, or you did have an excellent job and understand that if you did it once, you could do it again. Participate in your own life, be active and aggressive in seeking out things that will bring you joy and boost your self-esteem and confidence.

You cannot sit back and always let other people dictate the way you feel. When you seek positive information and start reminding yourself that you are good enough and that you are worth it, you determine what happiness and success look like for you. Stop comparing yourself to other people. Stop allowing others to bring you down.

Do not get jealous or have negative feelings towards someone because they have something that you don't. Instead, be happy for them and focus on what you can do for yourself. And when you have more confidence in yourself, your worth, and your abilities, you will begin to feel better. Once you start to appreciate your little accomplishments and acknowledge the little things in life that you are doing well, and focus on them, they will continue to grow and start to overthrow any negative thoughts you were having.

Sometimes low self-esteem could be caused by body image, weight, or the way you see yourself. Everyone is unique in their own way. If genetics are causing you to have a specific look about yourself, embrace it and become comfortable in your skin. If body image is an issue for you, how can you change the way you feel about yourself? Think about what you can do to change or control it. Are you eating healthy? Are you exercising? Are you doing the things that you can control? Are there things in your wardrobe that can be altered? Can you wear different clothes, or can you do your hair another way?

Consider changing up your style and your look. Are there ways you can do this? There are things you can control. Consider getting out of the routine of doing the same thing all the time. Changing your appearance on the outside can have a significant impact on how you feel on the inside. Have you ever heard the saying *when you look good, you feel good*? How you think about yourself is most important. Figure out what would help you feel more comfortable in your own skin, and don't worry about what other people will think about you.

Do whatever it takes to create a healthy level of self-esteem. You are unique; there is no one else like you. So, yes, you may look a little different; we all look different. But, if we all looked the same, the world would be really boring.

Start to believe in yourself and become more confident. The way you do this is by learning new things and trying new things so you can begin to believe new things about yourself. Read empowering books, watch inspirational videos, listen to educational podcasts, and become aware of what is possible for you. There is specialized knowledge out there right now you can use to improve yourself in any area of your life. The first step is deciding what you want to do; what it is you want in your life. Define a clear picture of what you want your life to look like, and then start learning what it will take to make it happen.

Have respect for your body and your mind, and be careful of what you're consuming. Don't fill your mind and your body with garbage. Be aware of the consequences listening to negative music can have on you. Music and programming with a lot of profanity will feed the negativity. Junk food, greasy foods, tobacco, and alcohol all contribute to the way you feel. The healthier you are, the better you treat your body and mind, the better you're going to feel, not just physically but mentally as well. Remember to drink plenty of water and get a proper amount of sleep so your body can perform to its maximum potential. You are going to feel healthier, have more energy, and boost your self-esteem in the process.

You will feel much better about yourself when you are consistently taking care of yourself over time. Drastic changes don't happen instantly; nothing happens overnight. Everything is a process. Know what you want, set your goals, and put your mind to them. Create an action plan and start to develop yourself in the areas of your life that you're not feeling great about right now. When you continue the good habit of taking care of yourself, the rewards will begin to appear, and the wait will have been well worth it.

If there is a specific area of your life where you're not feeling great, read books about it, watch shows on it, and learn how to improve that area of your life. Don't just let it keep bothering you without trying to improve it. The resources are out there. You have to put a little effort into seeking out the necessary resources, and you will be amazed at the information you can find.

If you are uncomfortable facing these challenges on your own, you can find a support group of other people who may have similar issues as what you're going through. Get a support system of people you can talk to openly about what's bothering you. Getting positive encouragement from others is a great way to lift your self-esteem to a level where you can feel good about yourself; you deserve it. Now it's time to take action.

Step 9 - Goals

This chapter is all about setting goals and ways to achieve the goals you set for yourself. You will understand why some people never set goals to begin with and how you can achieve anything you want if you set the goal and work towards it properly. We already talked about identifying your purpose, developing an optimistic mindset, confidence, courage, and a healthy self-esteem level. So, you should have a better idea about what you want to do with your time and energy and some of the things you want in your life.

Now that you are a more confident and courageous individual and more comfortable in your own skin, let's talk about setting some goals to achieve anything you want in your life. Hopefully, you've had some ideas pop into your head while reading the previous chapters and now you're ready to create an action plan.

There are several areas of your life where you will want to set goals. You will want to set health goals, financial goals, career goals, educational goals, family goals, spiritual goals, and monetary things that you want to acquire in your life. Whether it be a car, a house, a boat, or any other physical object you would like to have. Once you understand how to set goals effectively, the possibilities are endless.

So, keep those areas I just mentioned in mind because you're going to be able to apply this information to any of those areas in your life. Although the results of each goal will be different, the method of goal setting and achieving can work for all goals.

The first thing you need to do is identify what you want in each of the main areas of your life. Then write a list for each area. Set a timer for five minutes and dump all your ideas onto a piece of paper. Don't worry about how you will achieve these results, just put anything you want on the list. Then we will focus on getting specific in the next phase of the process.

After you have your list, you can start to set priorities. Which is most important? Number them in order of most important to least important. Then put a date for when you would like to accomplish each one. Setting a date for when you want to achieve them is especially important. There will also be different timeframes for each of your goals. You'll want to have daily, weekly, monthly, one-year, five-year, and ten-year goals. And possibly even farther out than that if you want.

Identify what's most achievable right now and put it on your daily or weekly goals list. And then look at those things that will take some time to accomplish and determine if you think it will take a month, five months, or a year to complete, then put it on the appropriate list.

Let's begin with an example of some health goals. Even if you are healthy right now, it's best to have a manageable plan to keep you on the right track if you want to stay that way. Even if it's something as simple as just eating better quality foods, less fast food, taking in fewer carbs and fats, or eating less sugar.

Then there is exercise. Do you have a current exercise routine, or do you fly by the seat of your pants and do it whenever the mood strikes you? Having a daily goal of getting your heart rate going is a good habit to have. Even if your daily goal is to walk at least one mile, do a certain amount of sit-ups or jumping jacks, or any other physical exercise, something is better than nothing. The key is to become consistent in whatever it is you decide to do. Make your goals realistic, manageable, and attainable so they will be easy to do, and you will have the best chance of successfully keeping with the plan.

And if you just set that small goal of doing a little bit of physical activity, in addition to eating healthy, you'll be working towards a bigger goal of losing a specific amount of weight. Or say you want to pack on some muscle, and you're lifting weights, and your goal is to bench press three-hundred pounds, but right now, you can only lift one-hundred pounds; you will have to set timeframe goals. Your goal for three months from now can be to get to one-hundred-fifty pounds, and maybe six months after that, you can reach your end goal of three hundred pounds. All goals are not immediately attainable, and specific goals will take time.

For example, if you want to lose thirty pounds within the next six months, write that date down. Then do the math to figure out how many pounds you need to lose per month. How many pounds do you need to lose per day? Then suddenly you realize; it means you would only need to lose five pounds per month. That is only a little more than one pound per week and only a few ounces per day if you are consistent throughout one hundred and eighty days.

Having a plan is one of the most important things you can do outside of setting the goal itself. Tracking your progress is another proven key to success.

Career goals can work hand in hand with your education goals. Let's say you want to be a computer programmer and work for Microsoft, but you only know a little bit about computers. The desired job may require you to understand how to do specific coding. If you want to learn how to write JavaScript or HTML code, you may need to take some courses. Then you do your research and realize that the coding course could be a six-month or one-year course. So that becomes a six-month or one-year goal; I want to know how to write enough code to get a job working for an IT company like Microsoft one year from today.

The above was just an example of how one desired outcome can require goals for multiple areas of your life. Once you know what you want, then you can prioritize it and create that vision. The key to it is to be specific. Become crystal clear on what you want.

So, if it is a car, you want to identify what kind of car it is, what color that car will be. Picture all the little details, envision yourself driving the car, and imagine how it will feel. Create a dream board with pictures of the exact vehicle you desire to have and hang it somewhere you will see it every day.

You want to keep your goals fresh in your mind. Write your goals down on a piece of paper and carry them with you in your pocket, and read them several times a day, preferably out loud and with enthusiasm; that is how you will attract these things to you. Your subconscious mind will be working towards helping you achieve these goals because your subconscious mind doesn't know if what you want is real or imaginary. And if you convince it that you already have these things, they will become real.

Once you decide what it is you want, it is crucial to understand why you want it. Keeping that reason why clearly in the forefront of your mind will keep you pushing forward when you are having a bad day or hit roadblocks, have setbacks or don't feel like picking yourself up out of bed in the morning. Because when you know why you want to do something, that will help motivate you and get you through when you want to quit. Because when you don't have a strong reason for doing something, it will be a lot easier to quit or give up.

There will be obstacles regardless of what the goal is. Depending on any given situation, you may face small hurdles or significant obstacles. Think ahead about what type of obstacles could show up and prepare yourself for them in advance. Identify what could get in your way and create a strategy of how to avoid that potential problem.

For example, when it comes to creating an exercise routine and your goal is to do it daily, what can come up to prevent you from following through with your plan? If you planned to do it at five o'clock every night, but you know there's a particular TV show that's going to come on at the same time, you may get distracted. So maybe you want to push the time back to when the show will be over. Whatever it is, when you can think ahead about what obstacles you will face, you can create your plan based around known distractions. If you currently have a full schedule, consider waking up earlier than usual to do your most important task before getting into your familiar routine.

By planning a time for when you will work on specific goals and committing to consistent action, you will be giving yourself the best chance of achieving your desired results. Making goals realistic and attainable and breaking them down into small, doable chunks will keep you from getting frustrated and abandoning them before seeing the results. When starting something new, it is essential to give it enough time to see the progress. Because once you do, it will motivate you and prove that what you are doing is working.

The amount of time you give yourself to achieve a specific goal can make a huge difference. If you have a huge goal, be sure to allow the appropriate amount of time to achieve it. Because if you try to accomplish a one-year sized goal in two months, you will most likely become frustrated and get discouraged.

Yes, you can have big goals, but you can't say, "I want to make a million dollars tomorrow" and then get mad when it doesn't happen. You can have that make a million dollars goal but understand that this may need to be a five-year or ten-year goal. When you have big goals, you want to break them down into smaller parts. What can you do to earn two thousand seven hundred and forty dollars every day? That is what it would take to earn one million dollars in one year. Brainstorm some ideas and research what jobs pay that kind of money or consider what business you can start that would make you this amount of money?

Can you create a twenty-dollar product and sell one hundred and thirty-seven of them every day? What if you could create a one-hundred-dollar product and sell twenty-eight of those every day? I think you get the point; you can play with numbers like this all day long. Think creatively about any result you are looking to achieve. Start with your end game, and then work your way backward. Working backward from the desired result is the same concept I used for losing a specific amount of weight. Break it down as small as you can, and you will arrive at what you need to do daily to hit your big goals.

There are several reasons most people don't set goals. Often, it is because a person doesn't believe they would ever be able to achieve any goal they set for themselves. Some of this comes from the conditioning of other people in their lives who have said, "you can never do this, or you will never be able to accomplish that, don't even bother trying," and the famous; "you are wasting your time." When a person has had family, friends, or teachers repeatedly telling them what they can't do, a lot of times, people start to believe it.

When you set manageable, realistic goals, the goals you set for yourself will be possible, regardless of what someone else may have told you. Some people don't want to see anyone else succeed because they have not succeeded at achieving their dreams or reaching their goals and want to hold someone else back. Please don't allow other people to steal your dreams and keep you from aiming high and setting goals. Believe in yourself. Just because someone else told you that you couldn't do something doesn't make it true.

The other reason why some people don't set goals is that they don't believe they deserve the result of the goal. All the previous chapters have been preparing you for this very moment. Because having a healthy level of self-esteem and the proper mindset will prevent you from becoming a victim of this type of thinking. Each topic in this book is related to goal setting in some way, shape, or form. If you don't have good self-esteem, you may not believe that you deserve to achieve the result of the thing you want, and without having confidence in yourself, you may never try anything new.

When someone thinks very little of themselves, they begin to doubt their capabilities in all areas of their lives. They don't believe they can ever achieve a healthy body or make a lot of money or attract the right mate to themselves, or they don't think they are smart enough to graduate and get that diploma, certificate, or degree. Setting goals gives you purpose and provides you with a reason to look forward. Having the correct type of goals can pull a person out of self-loathing and provide them with hope and optimism.

You are going to have days when you don't feel motivated to work towards your goals. I want you to understand that it's the best time to do the work when you don't feel motivated. Because doing the work will create motivation. Although you may not feel like doing it when you start, you will feel much better when you're done because you kept that promise to yourself, and you will have created momentum, which will motivate you to do it again tomorrow.

Be aware of the difference between being busy and actively working towards the accomplishment of a goal. Be intentional with your actions. Have an action plan that has you doing the most important things first. Because just being busy doesn't always count as work. When you have your goals written down, and I suggest writing them out on paper, although you may want to also keep them on your phone or computer, they become real. When you have your written goals in your pocket, it is easier to keep them fresh in your mind.

With our phones and computers, there are so many apps and files that things get lost and become forgotten. A piece of paper is a physical reminder to help keep what is most important to you fresh in your mind. When your goals are written down, every time you pull that paper out, whether it's on purpose or just because it comes out with your money, read it and remind yourself what you're supposed to be doing and maybe even why you're doing it.

When you are applying all these strategies together, you will move closer to accomplishing your goals every day. You may not always see the results immediately because you may only be taking small daily steps, but the progress is happening. It is like if you've ever known someone who was three-hundred pounds and then you didn't see them for six months, and they lost fifty pounds, you would see a big difference. But if you see that person daily and they lost one pound per day, you probably wouldn't notice it.

The work is paying off. You may not notice it because it is happening in small increments. But when you begin to document your journey and track your progress, when you read that journal in a month, six months, or a year from now, you will see the amazing results you were able to achieve.

The documentation of your journey is a powerful tool. Keep track of what worked and what didn't so you can apply these learning experiences to other areas of your life. Once you see yourself accomplishing little goals, it will motivate you to set bigger and better goals. Whether it be a short-term or long-term goal, create your action plan and commit to making a little bit of progress every day.

Another thing that can increase your chances of sticking with your goal is to have an accountability partner. Find someone or a group of people who are also working towards a similar goal as yours. You can get together with them once a week to discuss each other's progress and then share what you plan to accomplish the following week. Doing this will give you a sense of accountability and the feeling that you are not alone on this journey. When you are only accountable to yourself, it is easy to make excuses and put things off, but it can be a powerful motivator when you give someone your word.

Find a way to reward yourself when you hit a milestone or accomplish a goal. The satisfaction of achievement is a great reward, but sometimes a small treat can go a long way. For example, when it comes to dieting, if you say, "I'm going to lose five pounds by the end of this month, and if I hit my goal, I'm going to have a cheat day and eat my favorite meal. Then I'm going back on my diet until I hit my next milestone." And the thought of that next cheat meal will be what keeps you going through the hunger pains and weak moments you will have along the way.

A solid way to avoid getting off track is to lay out your plan for the next day the night before. When it comes to dieting, consider planning and cooking your meals for an entire week. Preparation is a big key to staying on track because if you wake up in the morning and then say, "okay, what am I going to do today? Or what am I going to eat today?" There is a good chance you will get sidetracked and get caught up doing busy work or eating something quick and easy that won't help with accomplishing your goals. And then you may never get around to doing what is most important.

When you have a written plan and a schedule for yourself and prioritize your time, it's more likely you will accomplish your goal. Everybody is busy, and your spare time is limited. So, the last thing you want to do is waste that precious time by doing something that is not important.

You may not have thought about setting important goals for yourself before, so in the beginning, it may take some extra time, but it's worth it. This process might even take you a couple of hours, but once you write it down and you get your plan in place, your written plan will save you a lot of time later because you're not wasting time on stuff that isn't important anymore.

Now that you understand how goal setting and achieving works, you will focus specifically on what matters most. Avoid wasting time, like when you didn't have anything specific to do, and you were going about your day, doing whatever happens. After you get your daily goals accomplished, relax, and have some fun, watch tv, and chill. When you discipline yourself to do what you need to do early in the day, you can enjoy the night guilt-free, knowing that you got a lot done today.

The rewards for all your hard work will start to show up, be patient with yourself. I know you can do it. You may be tempted to put something off or skip a day sometimes. Procrastination is a big thief of time. So, in the next chapter, I will help you understand how to avoid procrastination and get more done than you ever imagined was possible, even when you don't feel like doing anything.

How important is it for you to accomplish your goals, and what are you willing to sacrifice to make it happen?

Step 10 - Procrastination

What causes you to procrastinate? You may struggle with accomplishing some of your goals because of procrastination but don't feel alone; this is an issue many people struggle with. There are so many different things fighting for our attention. Distractions are everywhere. Considering how many things we can do with our phones, it is super easy to get sidetracked from what we initially set out to do. Procrastination is hard to avoid in some cases, but if you have strategies and know-how to overcome it, you can do it, and that is what this chapter is all about.

Procrastination is a thief of your time and something that takes away from your productivity. Delaying the action needed to achieve your goals and resisting what you know needs to be done is the most basic form of procrastinating. How often do you put off doing your most important task for something less essential?

Let's take a look at some of the most common reasons people procrastinate. For some, they are scared, have anxiety, or other specific fears. They may have a fear of failure, fear of rejection, or a fear of embarrassment. Depending on what the goal or task is will have a lot to do with why someone will find every excuse in the book to avoid doing what needs to get done.

Many people have a vision of wanting to be perfect when they do something, and if they're not doing it perfectly, they are constantly starting over. Remember this phrase; *done is better than perfect*. Perfectionists often never finish what they start because, in their minds, it's not okay just to do a good job; it needs to always be perfect. Focus on doing the best you can, get it done, and move on. Perfection is overrated.

If you have a fear of rejection, you may hesitate to put yourself out there. If you're embarrassed about the way you look or have low self-esteem, as we talked about in a previous chapter, you may be hesitant to go to a gym and physically exercise in front of other people. This fear may even cause you to have anxiety about going out and walking around your neighborhood for exercise because you worry about what people might say to you or think of you. Talking yourself out of doing what you need to do is easy. Instead of doing your exercise, it's a lot easier to sit on the couch and watch TV.

When you become committed to avoiding the path of least resistance, you will get more done than you ever imagined was possible. Begin to face your fears. Here is an acronym for the word fear that I believe will help you. FEAR – False Evidence Appearing Real. Sometimes we get ourselves so worked up over what we think is true, but it is often just a figment of our imagination. Unless you are doing something that can literally kill you, try to avoid letting fear stop you from doing what needs to be done.

Having big goals and wanting to accomplish big things requires effort. If it were easy, everybody would do it. Don't wait to become inspired. In the beginning, you may have to force yourself to do what needs to be done, but it gets easier every time you do it. Getting started is the hardest part. Doing new things will require you to develop new habits. I have a whole chapter on habits in my book *Self-Help for At-Risk Teens*. New habits take time to develop. Studies show that it takes at least twenty-one consecutive days of doing something to create most habits, and on the flip side, twenty-one consecutive days of not doing something to break a habit. So don't get discouraged if things don't happen right away. Taking tiny steps every single day is essential.

Having a goal and knowing why you're doing it is a powerful tool in helping you to avoid procrastinating. Every minute, every hour, and every day you put something off, it's going to make it that much harder to get going. The timing won't always be perfect. The time to get started on something important is right now. Start by doing it a little bit, and then increase the amount of time or the amount of effort you put into achieving your goal or finishing a task.

The key to making progress every single day is to focus on the most important goal or task you have and doing that first every day before there is any chance of getting distracted. When you make doing this a habit, that sense of accomplishment will pull you through the rest of your day. And even if you get nothing else done throughout the day, you'll at least have done the most important thing. And then, the next day, focus on the next most important thing on your list. Every day you do the biggest, most challenging thing first. And if it's an ongoing project, you break it down into small chunks, and you do one piece every day. The more you do this, the more comfortable you'll become with the process.

If you've had the habit of procrastinating for a while, it will be harder to break. Get clear on exactly what it is you need to do and have a plan. Try to avoid getting shiny object syndrome. For example, when you sit down at the computer to get some work done, suddenly an email pops up, so you check your email, and then before you know it, you're checking Facebook. After you finish scrolling through all your messages, it is lunchtime, and you never got to do any of the work you initially logged on to do.

Allowing every little thing that catches your eye to get you sidetracked will keep you from being productive and getting your most important tasks accomplished. That is why it's essential to set a schedule and do the most important thing first. There will always be time to check email, social media, and text messages later. Prioritizing what is most important to you will require discipline.

If you create your schedule the night before, you will know what you need to do first the next day. If you let too much of the day pass by before getting to your most important task, it makes way for distractions to slow you down and gives you too much time to create excuses for why it can wait until tomorrow. So, before you check email or other messages, get some work done on what matters most. If it's a big project, but you don't have a lot of time to dedicate to it every day, commit to working on it for at least one hour per day. Some days, you may increase the amount of time you can spend, but you will have at least made some progress each day.

So if you've had the problem of procrastination in the past, don't focus on it anymore. Just concentrate on taking daily action to move in the direction of accomplishment and start to tell yourself that you are no longer a procrastinator. Decide today that you will no longer procrastinate. Make the decision and use your self-discipline to do it long enough for it to become a habit.

If you have a bad day or miss a day, get back on it the next day. It is up to you to do what's important to you. No one's going to do it for you. When you have a strong reason for getting something done, it will overpower the temptation to resist doing what is necessary.

One of the most significant ways people procrastinate is simply waiting until the last minute to do everything. For example, when someone has a project that's due on Friday, a lot of times people wait until Thursday to start, and then they're rushing to finish, and if it gets done, it will be at the last minute and undoubtedly not as good as it could have been if they took their time and didn't rush. If this happens to you, start to trick yourself. If you have a project due on Friday, tell yourself it's due on Wednesday, and start working on it on Monday. And if you do a little bit more on Tuesday, by Wednesday, it could be finished, and you're two days early. This way, in case you have any issues, you'll have an extra day or two as a buffer.

Tricking yourself is also helpful if you have the terrible habit of always being late. Whether it's late to school, work, meeting with friends, getting to appointments on time, or whatever the case may be, if always being late is an issue, here are a couple of ways to prevent it from happening.

Move your clocks fifteen minutes ahead of the correct time. This way, you are doing everything fifteen minutes before you usually would. Adjusting your clocks is also helpful with waking up on time in the morning.

If you have to be somewhere at six o'clock, tell yourself you have to be there at five-thirty. This way, you leave a little earlier, and you get there a little earlier, and in case you are running late, you will still technically be on time. These are helpful ways to create the habit of being early.

There is a difference between procrastinating and planning. Taking time to do research and think about how you want something to turn out is perfectly understandable. When too much research and planning keep from getting the actual work done, it becomes a problem. Sometimes it is best to start on a project with what you already know and figure out what else you need to learn after you get started. Then you can go back and gather more info or practice a specific step that isn't working.

If you don't have space to work, do you need to clear something out? When it comes to exercising or any other project that requires a dedicated space, are you putting it off because you don't have the room to do it? If so, think about clearing out your garage or your basement or organizing your bedroom to give yourself the space you need to do the work. Dedicate some time to reorganizing the areas you have and create the space you need. Having a productive environment can make it easier to get started and help motivate you to get more done.

Think about accomplishing those things that are the most important to you and how your life will be different when you do. When you envision yourself achieving the results of your goals, it will help you overcome any procrastination you may be dealing with.

Your time is more valuable than money. Once you understand the value of your time, it will become clear that the only way to maximize your most valuable asset is to avoid procrastination. Do your best to make the most of every minute you have. Don't let less important things distract you anymore. I know you can do this. Make the commitment today that you will no longer be a procrastinator.

Let go of your past negative experiences, let go of what people think about you, and whatever else may be holding you back. Commit to getting the important stuff done first and declutter your life from anything that's slowing you down.

Overcoming procrastination is all about breaking old habits and creating new positive ones.

Step 11 - Positive Thinking

Positive thinking is going to tie together all the topics that we have covered over all the previous chapters and what we're going to cover in the next chapter, self-image. Without the ability to think positively, it will be challenging to achieve success in those other areas if you are constantly thinking negative about yourself and what's possible.

Being optimistic will give you the ability to believe good things can happen. If you don't have a positive mindset, you may never set goals for yourself. Positive thinking can't do everything for you, but it can do much more for you than having negative thinking. When you think negatively and don't think something is worth it, or you don't think you'll be able to achieve it or do whatever it is you want to do, you will give up before you ever get started. There is a famous saying that goes like this, *whether you think you can or think you can't, you're right.* What you are capable of starts in your mind.

If someone is pessimistic and they think everything is going to go wrong, they never bother trying. And if these pessimists never get started, they reaffirm their thoughts of fear, doubt, and worry. They justify their thinking by saying things like, "I know I couldn't have done that, or it was never going to work out anyway." They never allow themselves an opportunity to see what is possible.

You must have faith to see if something will work or not because it's hard to know if you're good at something or if you can do something if you never try. Which is why thinking positively and believing in the unknown is the first step towards all achievement.

Whether you are setting out to fulfill your purpose or want to go out and change the world in your unique way, or you simply want to help a few people, either way you must believe it's possible before getting started. The details of how it will happen may not be clear yet but having the belief of possibility is crucial. Trusting what you can't see will provide the motivation to get the ball rolling.

Your attitude is affected by your thoughts. Relationships, grades in school, job performance, faith in society, and so many other areas of our lives are directly affected by how we perceive the situation. And because we as humans have total control of our minds, we can change how we think about any situation at any time. If you are feeling conflicted, take time to learn more about the issue you're dealing with and if afterwards you feel negative, make the decision to let it go. Set this negativity free from your mind and no longer focus on it.

We attract what we focus on most. If success in your career is what you want, see yourself being successful. Please don't focus on how hard it will be to get your dream job. If graduating with a specific degree is what you desire, see yourself walking across the stage and being handed that coveted certificate. Try to avoid focusing on all the hard work it will take to get you to the finish line; focus on what you can control and take the process one day at a time.

Begin to see yourself living a life full of possibilities and opportunities, and don't allow other people to crush your dreams. When you believe in yourself it doesn't matter what other people think because you know yourself better than anybody. And as long as you don't allow outside forces to convince you otherwise, your dreams will remain alive. Start where you are and with what you have, and then improve on it. Get more resources and experiences that can help you get better at whatever you are trying to do. But most importantly, get started!

Using affirmations is a powerful way to develop positive thinking. Reaffirming to yourself positive thoughts, things you want to accomplish, possessions you wish to acquire, and changes you want to make will fill your mind with thoughts of possibility.

Affirming that you are going to hit your goals is as easy as writing it out on paper and then saying out loud; I will (fill in the blank) and say it with enthusiasm and conviction. For example, losing a specific amount of weight, achieving a particular grade in a class or making a specific sports team, or learning how to play an instrument. Repeat your statement several times per day out loud; "I am going to do this." And in addition to saying the affirmations, do the work. Practice, work hard and believe that you can accomplish your goals. Your subconscious mind will start to work towards it with you. And the more you see it, the more you hear it, the more you envision it, the more possible and real the result of your goal becomes.

Read stories of people who have overcome significant obstacles in their life to go on and achieve huge successes. There are plenty of inspirational stories available to give you the ability to realize that positive results are possible even for someone who is facing many challenges or adversities. Adversity can help a person grow.

Stay focused on the positive and don't get sucked into the negative. Because surrounding yourself with negativity and negative people is contagious and will eventually rub off on to you. But when you spend your time around positive people, and you're reading inspirational books, watching encouraging videos, and listening to empowering audio, you won't be able to resist the feelings of positivity. Constantly putting reassuring information into your mind will reaffirm what's possible for you and build your belief system.

All this positivity talk may be hard to believe at first if you are not used to having good things happen to you. If you have been surrounded by negativity for a long time, this will require a new way of thinking. The best part of turning this positive life fantasy into an actual reality is that it doesn't have to cost any money. You can start by listening to uplifting podcasts, watching motivational YouTube videos, and getting inspirational books from the free library. Most libraries now have mobile apps that allow you to read eBooks and listen to audiobooks on your phone, tablet, or computer. The choice is yours. You can choose any one of these options, or you can do them all.

Start with fifteen minutes per day and then add more time as you become more comfortable with this new way of spending your time. Filling your mind with positive thoughts will help to develop your confidence and boost your self-esteem. Step into your power and do what will make you happy even if it requires you to get out of your comfort zone because that is where all your dreams are possible.

I encourage you to surround yourself with positive people and continue to fill your mind with positive information. Negativity will sabotage your progress. Thinking positive can be hard to do when being surrounded by negativity. It is not easy to shift your mindset from being negative to positive, but it can happen. You can do it if you actively work towards it and believe a positive lifestyle is possible by putting the correct information into your mind and believing in yourself.

When you think back on all the topics that have been covered in this book, they all work hand in hand with positive thinking. Not a single area of your life can benefit from negative thinking. The more positive you think, the easier it will be when you are developing your goals and setting out to do something you have never done before.

Positive thinking will change your life if you let it. If you consciously develop an optimistic outlook, if you make it a habit of looking at the bright side of every situation, if you can create the habit of putting positive information into your mind, only positive can come out. That's the way it works, positive in and positive out.

Think back to the chapter about personal responsibility and not making excuses and being positive and optimistic about achieving the things you want in your life. Think about taking control of your life and being responsible for what you have in your life. You control your destiny through your ability to think and act in a way that will move you closer to becoming the person you desire to be.

Appreciate the opportunities you have even if you don't think what you have is much. Being grateful is a powerful way to get positive thoughts going through your mind. Being thankful for what you do have and not focusing on the things you don't have will allow you to appreciate the little things in life. There is magic in simplicity.

Do your best to avoid the negative things that are around you in your daily life and focus on looking for the positive in all situations. Start by trying to avoid all negativity for one week and see how much different you feel. Carry your affirmations on a piece of paper and read them several times per day. Listen to educational audio or podcasts while you are commuting instead of music. Try to read a few pages of an uplifting book every day. Challenge yourself to only look for the positive in the world around you. Fill your mind with positive thoughts; I know you can do it. Just work towards it a little bit every day. I know it's possible. I know it's not easy, but I also know it's worth the effort.

Step 12 - Self-Image

Our self-image affects everything we do in one way or another. It affects the way we think and how we see ourselves, and it affects our actions based on our beliefs about ourselves.

Your self-image is tied directly to your belief system. Your belief about yourself and what you think you are capable of have been influenced by what other people throughout your life have told you. And if you allow it, these beliefs can hold you back from going after what you want out of life. Sometimes we get hung up on believing what other people are saying when we need to trust ourselves and our instincts.

When we believe in ourselves and what we're capable of, we come to know ourselves better, and we develop our intuition. When we become more knowledgeable about who we are, we begin to believe new things about ourselves, enhancing our self-image.

Start to do more positive and encouraging things for yourself. Develop your self-awareness so you can see yourself in a more positive light. Our self-image is the way we see ourselves and not the way other people see us. We can control how we see ourselves. There are ways to boost your confidence, self-esteem, and faith in your abilities. Every topic in this book has been a building block towards creating an overall healthier self-image.

If you don't believe you will be able to do great things, you probably won't ever try. If you see yourself in a negative way, this thinking can hinder you from making the necessary changes to improve the quality of your life. Make an effort to get out of your same old routine and create some new habits. Change is not easy, but it's worth it if you're doing it for the right reasons.

Don't allow someone else's view of you affect the way you see yourself. You can't change what other people think about you, but you can change the way you see yourself, and that is what's most important. You can change the people you surround yourself with, but you're never going to be able to get away from yourself. Take control of what you believe about the person you see in the mirror. Compliment yourself and think encouraging thoughts. Do things that will make you happy and treat yourself the way you deserve to be treated.

You are cable of seeing yourself in a new way. Consider starting a hobby you have always dreamed of doing. Read encouraging books, find a job you like, or spend time with people who make you happy. The most significant changes happen on the inside but treat yourself to new clothes and a haircut if it will enhance the way you feel about yourself. The journey of personal improvement is a customized experience. Do what you think will create happiness and gratification in your life.

If you don't value yourself, you're going to lack the confidence and motivation to try new experiences. I encourage you to think better of yourself, feel positive about yourself, and place a higher value on your self-worth. Regardless of your age, you always have the ability to change not only the way you see yourself but the way you present yourself to the world around you. There are so many things that you can control about your life. Now is the time to take advantage of all opportunities that will propel you into the future.

Sometimes we don't realize how good our lives are until we see less fortunate people. Consider volunteering at a homeless shelter, visiting an orphanage, or find a way to donate some of your time to helping those who are less fortunate. Because when you are helping other people, you will feel good, and it can help you realize how valuable you can be. If you're not comfortable volunteering, maybe you could donate some of your old clothes or donate money to a worthy cause or do anything that will help you see a new side of yourself.

You can help people by doing things that benefit them and make you feel better about yourself. These are all ways to build your self-image and allow you to see yourself in a better way and in a more positive light.

Changing your habits and routines will not be easy at first, but it's worth the effort. If right now, the things you're doing are not bringing you happiness or satisfaction, or you're struggling to find your purpose, or you're not living up to your full potential, the only way to change this is to do something different.

Therefore, I am encouraging you to look at what you're doing with your time, energy, money, and effort and start to think about how you can improve your habits and what you're doing every day. Starting from the time you wake up until you go to bed, have goals, have an agenda, plan your day, plan your life, make time to do what is most important to you.

If you get stuck in a routine that doesn't allow you to be happy, it is up to you to change it. People can tell you how to do things, but they can't or won't do it for you in most cases. There are certain things that only you can do yourself, and changing the way you see yourself is one of them. If you apply the strategies you have learned throughout this book into your life, there is no doubt that your self-image will improve. Because the more you begin to practice positive habits, the more you will see yourself in a positive way.

Our new reality in a post-pandemic world is bringing change and new opportunities for everyone. We all have a chance to start fresh and create a new version of ourselves. Are you going to reinvent yourself or go back to living the same way you were before twenty-twenty?

Think about what you want your new life to look like and create an action plan for how you will make it happen. Your plan should include goals for all areas of your life where you can see room for improvement. And the more success you achieve, the better you will feel. Begin with small achievements and then build upon them. When you believe in yourself, you will be amazed at what you can accomplish.

So, I encourage you to take a good look at what you're putting into your mind, how you are living, what opinions you are listening to, how you are spending your time, and who you are spending it with. Are you willing to make the necessary changes? Become excited about the new you.

Don't waste time; start taking action now! Become excited about your future. You can become much more than you are right now. You are young, and you have so much room to grow. Your future is bright. Believe in yourself, set your goals, and work hard to achieve them. Commit to becoming a better person, and the world around you will become better.

Congratulations on finishing this book! Good luck in achieving everything you set your mind to and reach out to me if I can help in any way. I'm looking forward to hearing about your success story!

I would love to hear your testimonial and get your feedback on how this book has helped you. Please review this book on the website from which you purchased it. If it was a gift, reach out to the person who gave it to you, thank them, and let them know what you thought of this information, and please ask them to leave the review for you. Please tell your friends about this book and share it on social media. Thank you.

To assist you in continuing your personal development, I invite you to join the free self-help eBook of the week club. Get started today by visiting www.TheSelfHelpCompany.com

Book Excerpt - Self-Help for At-Risk Teens

SELF-HELP FOR AT-RISK TEENS

OVERCOME THE ODDS AND LIVE THE LIFE OF YOUR DREAMS

BEN POVLOW

Introduction

I was raised in unfortunate circumstances, but I believe the way I handled it made things much worse than they should have been. I now realize my life as a young adult had been the consequence of my poor decisions as a teenager. I was not prepared to become an adult. The main goal of this book is to teach you the things I wish I had known when I was your age—how to become independent, take care of yourself and avoid the dangerous pitfalls associated with being *at-risk*.

I have since changed my life for the better, but I can't change my past. What I can control is what I do with all the knowledge I've gained from my experiences. I will talk about what has worked for me and the areas of my life where I wish I would have done things differently. I am choosing to share this wisdom with you, so you can avoid making the same mistakes I made.

If I could go back and change my life, this book is what I would use as a guide. Throughout this book, you will learn a wide range of information that will help you get from where you are to where you want to go in your life. Everything I talk about in this book is based on personal experiences and self-taught knowledge. These are not things I learned in a traditional classroom. I am combining my street smarts and common sense, mixed with a wide range of practical life experiences, and proven self-help and personal development strategies to give you an education like no one else can.

The first time I picked up a self-help book, my life was changed forever. When I realized I could change the course of my life by changing what I was putting into my mind, it was game on. I turned off the radio and put on an audiobook. I turned off the TV and started reading inspirational books. It started with small changes, and before I knew it, I was hooked.

I started going to seminars of the most recognizable names in self-improvement. For several years I followed these leaders around the country, soaking up their knowledge and investing a lot of money into learning how to become the best version of myself I could be.

My journey of personal improvement started fourteen years ago. I began by changing my self-image and focusing on becoming a better person. I overcame my limiting beliefs and began to create a vision for my future. I went on to develop skills in leadership, team building, coaching, public speaking, sales, and how to make money on the internet. I became good enough to start conducting seminars and teaching others what I was learning.

If this is the first book you are reading on personal improvement, welcome to the journey of a lifetime. Self-discovery is one of the most exciting things you will ever experience. Once you realize what you're truly capable of, your life will never be the same. Strive to live up to your true potential. I know it's possible and I know you can do it.

Learning how to overcome the odds and create a better life for yourself is a choice anyone can make. The life skills and personal development strategies I'll be sharing will give you the knowledge you need to get from where you are now to where you want to go in life. I believe in you. Just by holding this book, you have already taken the first step. Congratulations!

Contents

Chapter 1 - What is Putting You at Risk?

Chapter 2 - The Effects of Being at Risk

Chapter 3 - How Anger Affects You

Chapter 4 - Understanding Grief and Loss

Chapter 5 - Adapting to Your Living Situation

Chapter 6 – Friendship Qualities

Chapter 7 - Your Physical Well-Being

Chapter 8 - The Dangers of Drugs and Alcohol

Chapter 9 - The Price of Trouble

Chapter 10 - Developing Your Character

Chapter 11 - Becoming Aware of Your Habits

Chapter 12 - Taking Care of Yourself

Chapter 13 - Hobbies and Ways to Spend Your Time

Chapter 14 - Technology - Make It Work for You

Chapter 15 - Money - Make It, Save It, and Invest It

Chapter 16 - Self-Development Strategies

Self-Help for At-Risk Teens is available through all major online book retailers.

About The Author

Ben Povlow was born in Philadelphia, PA. After growing up as an at-risk youth, while still a young adult, he continued to struggle to break free of his negative environment. He wanted a better life but didn't know how to achieve it. When he was twenty-eight years old, he became aware of self-help and personal development materials that would transform him in a way he never knew was possible.

He went on to improve the quality of his life by reading books, listening to audio trainings, and going to seminars of the most recognizable names in self-improvement. He followed these leaders around the country for several years, soaking up their knowledge and investing a lot of money into learning how to become the best version of himself he could be.

Ben believes we all have the power to change our circumstances through the way we think, act, and see ourselves. He has overcome many obstacles in his life and believes that if he can do it, anyone can.

He is now living the life of his dreams. He is married and lives with his wife, Kathi, and stepdaughter, Katelyn, in a quiet suburb in central North Carolina. Ben has committed himself to improve the lives of others by sharing his knowledge and experience. He is an inspiring motivational public speaker, a certified life coach, author, and business owner. You can learn more about Ben, his company, and services by visiting www.TheSelfHelpCompany.com

www.ingramcontent.com/pod-product-compliance
Lightning Source LLC
Chambersburg PA
CBHW071856070526
44583CB00016B/1718